COAT ON A STICK

Late Poems

An agèd man is but a paltry thing,
A tattered coat upon a stick, unless
Soul clap its hands, and sing, and louder sing
For every tatter in its mortal dress.

W. B. YEATS, "Sailing to Byzantium"

COAT ON A STICK

Late Poems

ROLFE HUMPHRIES

INDIANA UNIVERSITY PRESS

BLOOMINGTON & LONDON

For John,
For Clare,
and
For Winifred

ACKNOWLEDGMENTS

The following poems have been published in periodicals or books as listed here: "Ballade of Wolfville" in Introduction to *Wolfville Yarns*, Kent (Ohio) University Press, 1968; "Belmont" in *Time* Magazine, May 30, 1968; "Silence, Godhead" in *United Church Herald*, 1969; "Contra Naturam," "Beardmanica," "Success Story" in *Denver Quarterly*, Summer, 1968; "Cymric Places," "Coat on a Stick," "Deepening Shades" in the *Chicago Tribune* Sunday Poetry Page, June 8, 1969; "Frisbee," "The Cedar Waxwing" in *The New Yorker*, 1969; "With Garb of Proof," "A Song for Mortimer" in *Poetry*, Chicago, March, 1969; "The Chillblain Indians" in the *Rocky Mountain Herald*, 1968; *La Cousine* in *New Statesman* (England), December 10, 1968; "Arachne, Penelope" in *Poetry Northwest* (University of Washington), Spring 1969; "The Screaming Meemies" in *The Nation*, May 5, 1969; "Camano Island" in *Malahat Review*, 1969; "The Spear Not Broken" and "The Ways of the Water, Part I and Part II" ["Water Course"], *Colorado Quarterly*, Spring 1969.

CONTENTS

A PREFATORY NOTE

Most of these poems have been written since February, 1967, when we came to California, although a few were done in 1966. They are presented in substantially chronological order. The reader who might be interested will find additional information as to the provenance and techniques of each poem in the Notes at the back of the book.

Some of these poems have appeared in periodicals, to which acknowledgments are made elsewhere. I am also indebted to my sister (Mrs. Ivor J. Davies) for help with the typing of the text, and for valuable suggestions about its content.

ROLFE HUMPHRIES

Woodside, California
April, 1969

THE BEARDMANICA

(for Ron Gordon)

> *... let Humphreys, house of Humphreys,*
> *rejoice with the Beardmanica, a curious bird.*
> —*Christopher Smart*

A curious bird indeed. I find
No reference in Audubon
To any creature of his kind.
Therefore, imagination

Must fill the blank. Let's see. His crest,
Made, not of feathers, but of hair,
Has slipped between his chin and vest,
A sort of Salmon Chase affair.

His nesting habits are uncouth.
His mating-call is like a bark.
He mates for life, in early youth,
But does so only after dark.

The plumage shades from beige to dun,
Or, it may be, from gray to taupe.
Of field-marks there are almost none
Except the bright vermilion cope

Spread when he flies from east to west.
The eggs are oval-shaped and brown
With spotted zigzags, and the nest
Is sometimes lined with mullein-down,

And sometimes not. He likes to eat
Grubs, worms, bugs, ants, rye, spelt, and maize;
He scorns, however, Shredded Wheat
And any grist commercials praise.

I could go on, but never mind.
Some scholars, blest with little wit,
Claim he is really just a tit.
They must be absolutely blind.

I don't believe a word of it.

MORNING, OLD STYLE

It is five of the clock
And the sun is apace
On his journey. Fie sluggards
Who loll in their beds!

The steeple bells ring
For the people to pray
To the saint of the day.
The streets fill with folk
And the highways are stores
With wandering wights,
Farers and followers,
Bagmen and boolies.

The scholars are up
And are going to school.
For truants' correction
The rods are at ready.
The maids are at milking,
The tillers at plough,
The wheel whirleth gay
While the mistress is by.

The capons and chickens
Cluck at their meal
Chucked over sill
To be served out of door.

The hogs grunt the ground
In pen and in sty,
By trough and by wallow,
Till they're slopped with their swill.

Blind Leary is up
For his cake and his cup,
With his bow and his fiddle,
His dance and his song,
And the door of the alehouse
Unlocks for good fellows.

The hounds bell their crying
After the hare
And horse and foot follow.
Well on his way
The traveler goes,
The weather is fair
And he walks with good cheer.

Merrily whistles
The carter his dray horse
And the boy with his sling
Is alert to be flinging
Stones at the crows.

FUGUE FOR
THE VERNAL EQUINOX
(for Porter Dickinson)

Snow falls now as evening falls,
But better days should creep in soon.
The sad light of late afternoon
Lengthens, very slowly.

Better days should soon creep in,
Snow be loss, and sun be gain;
Over hill and valley
Brown give way to gold and green.

Sun be gain and snow be loss,
Sun be more and snow be less.
Better days should soon be here,
And the afternoon's late air
Ever so little warmer, daily.

So, while exception dwells,
Over valleys, over hills,
Snow falls now as evening falls.

BALLADE OF WOLFVILLE

Nigh forgotten are Boggs and Tutt,
Texas Thompson, and Faro Nell
(Lookout for Cherokee Hall, who cut
The cards and shuffled and dealt as well),
Enright, Doc Peets, the clientele
Who went to the O.K. Grill for chow—
Toll for them all the passing-bell;
Wolfville is less than a ghost town now.

The Bird Cage Opera House is shut,
Not one Red Stocking Demoiselle
With a can-can kick or a cake-walk strut
Captures a ranch-hand Beau Brummel,
Casting enchantment, glamour, spell,
Over the footlights to endow
Nights with the music of Philomel—
Wolfville is less than a ghost town now.

Empty as trough or water-butt,
The Red Light Bar is a hollow shell.
Dust and sand fill the wagon rut
Where Monte, usually drunk as hell,
Drove the stagecoach; the cowboys' yell
Fades to silence, and steer and cow
Bawl no more where the gophers dwell—
Wolfville is less than a ghost town now.

L'envoi

Sheriff, serve, as the times compel,
Doom's writs and warrants, but still allow
One tear to fall where the last chip fell—
Wolfville is less than a ghost town now.

BELMONT

But where are the élite?
                     The Schoenbergs made
Their money honestly enough, in trade,
In trolley cars, in diamonds, bonds, or beer,
Banking or railroads, well-established here
By the mid-eighties, in an atmosphere
Of opulence, unquestionably graced
With what their times and peers would call good taste,
Arbiters of suburban etiquette,
Leaders of the town-and-country set.
They learned to adapt themselves to wearing spats,
Frock coats, striped morning trousers, bowler hats,
They learned to give high teas, to ride to hounds,
To keep within the proper meets and bounds,
Were public-spirited, would patronize,
Most lavishly, the decent charities;
Noblesse oblige. Somewhere along the line
The name was changed. What's wrong with that? That's fine,
They earned the privilege. Give them all their due,
But—weren't they still the least bit *parvenu,*
The least bit not quite Mayflower, F.F.V.,
A trace this side of true gentility,
A *soupçon,* a *sous-soupçon,* just below
The absolute apogee of *comme il faut?*
They did improve the breed, they kept alive
The sport of kings, so that in 1905

The naming of this racecourse set the crown
Of laurel on their virtuous renown,
As beautiful, as elegant a setting
As one could ever hope to find for betting.

But where are the aristocrats?
                                    Don't try
To find them in this rabble, this *canaille*,
These *sans-culottes* in shirtsleeves, *sans*, *aussi*,
The least investiture of quality.
Off the Long Island Railroad cars they swarm
With *Morning Telegraph* or *Racing Form*
And *Armstrong's Scratch Sheet*, pouring towards the gates
Beside which other literature awaits
As benefice, whose fain purveyors call
In accents more than audible by all,
"Jack's Little Green Card!", "Clocker Lawton!!", "Hey,
Got that Daily Double again today!!!"
(Don't trust these men, no matter how sincere
Solicitude may cause them to appear.)

What's all the rush? Slow down, let's wait a bit
Behind the stands, relax and sit,
Pause for a moment, take our ease
Under the over-arching trees,
Find a good bench, from which to view
Lawn, gardens, mall and avenue
Along which move the ebb, the flow
Of people passing to and fro

In shadow and sun, by elm or oak,
A gentler-seeming kind of folk,
More leisurely, as if their ways,
Inherited from better days,
Knew mildness, and the atmosphere
Held in suspension, even here,
A sense of ceremonial,
Of courtesy, of ritual,
As if even here, unconsciously,
We moved in grave amenity,
Or dwelt in grace, as if the air
Bespoke us laudable and fair.

"Riders up!" The bugle sounds First Call.
All eastward streams the rank processional.

But where are the patricians?
                              Cool it, Mac!
"The horses," Cappy says, "are on the track."

Let our eyes close, our memories watch again
Fields of our favorites, from Amblecane
To Zev, parading to the post, the bright
Silk stable-colors shining in the light—
Light blue, brown cap; all scarlet; white with green
Collar and cuffs, white cap; aquamarine,
Gold W, encircled, on the back;
Blue and white blocks; cerise, white diamonds; black
With yellow hoops; orange, black cap.
                              Behold

Black Servant, Brynlimah, Black Prince, Black Gold,
Co-Educator, Equipoise, Dark Star,
Dark Secret, and—that tourist!—Epinard,
Faireno, Kelso, Gallahadion,
Jim Dandy, Gallant Fox, Top Flight, Whichone,
And one we need not call by name, the get
Of Fair Play from Mahubah; and Regret,
Noor, Sergeant Byrne, Ponder, and Petrotude,
Miss Merriment, My Lovely, Singing Wood
(Bay colt, by Royal Minstrel out of Glade),
Cochise, Count Fleet, King Saxon, Cavalcade,
Three fillies, Sorrow and Song and Rust—remember?—
And Scarlet Oak, Right Royal, and Red Ember,
Nashua, Swaps, and Sting, and Twenty Grand,
Wise Counsellor, Whirlaway, and Yellow Hand,
Yurup, another gray one, Native Dancer—

Where are the ones with breeding?
                              Here's our answer
At last, in bright decorum going by
With the bloom on them, and the heads held high,
In all their delicate, fastidious, proud
Grace and perfection, stepping past the crowd.

SILENCE, GODHEAD

I can remember, some twenty years ago,
An episode of snow,
A fall so deep, traffic stopped everywhere,
Not only land, sea, air,
But even underground,
With stillness so profound
That lying in the dark, awake, I knew
Silence was more than mere absence of sound:
Silence was energetic, positive,
Dynamic, with a vital force, alive,
An entity.

And this comes back to me
Twenty years later as analogy
While pondering Lucretius, where he dwells
Upon the nature of the gods and tells
Of their serene repose, far, far above
Frivolities like mercy, justice, love;
Or even sillier stunts, which gratified
(Job 38–41) that King of Pride
Ancient of days, Braggart, whose neesings throw
Light over the world, Leviathan-hooker,—oh
Majesty, glory, beauty? Never so;

Not as compared with those calm presences
Who dwell almost—not quite—
Beyond the shores of light,
The flaming ramparts of the world, who are
Material—best not say *Barely so*
Considering what vital force they keep
Within themselves, how concentrated, deep,
Active and positive—serene repose
Brought to perfection. This must truly be
Godhead, divinity.
——Let us aspire.

THE SPEAR NOT BROKEN

The squares are frightened guys.
Some of them, for a while,
Affect the other style,
Almost chameleon-wise.

This raises questions: what
About that lone, uncouth
Raft-loving island youth?
Was Huck a square, or not?

Odysseus? Homeward bound,
Insistent so, he found
No siren-song, no charms
Of the bright goddess-arms,

No circean wand or wiles
Could block or overcome
His faring toward his home,
Strangest of all the isles.

Back to our world again—
Not all our squares are men
Of passion, but submit
With all too little wit

To "Let what will be, be,"
Or "Hearts asleep in the deep"—
For them no mimicry
Of anything but sheep:

Pious Aeneases,
Utterly boring, whom
We treat with merciless
Consignment to their doom.

So for ourselves, we might
Conclude—"Let there be light."

SUCCESS STORY

Listen, my children, and you'll be told
Of a man who got rich, but not from gold.

Our hero, heroic as well could be
Taught Phys. Ed. at the U. of C.

Call him by name—Dwight Farraday,
Born in Yuma, but raised in Wray.

His major responsibility
Mountaineering 8a and b,

Leading the hikers, on the trail,
Or more cross-country, through sand and shale.

"Gold in them hills?" he thought. How trite!
Dwight had a better idea, all right.

So he went to the Geiger counter store
And bought a dozen, or maybe more.

These, when the boys got back to town
At the end of the day, and were stripping down,

Before their showers, he would apply,
With special note, to their umbilici.

His ears agog and his eyes aglint
For a hint of the uraniferous lint.

Where there seemed promise, he'd have them stay
Under observation, oh, half a day,

While he made the best of his happy find,
Drew off, extracted, vacuumed, mined,

Delved, exhausted, and so grew rich,
The pioneering son of a bitch.

BALLADE AND SONNET
(Variations on a Theme)

THE BALLADE

I

How many times we have watched the second hand
Going around the dial's face, and always go
Back where it started from. We understand
How time can be obsessive, and a foe
Insistent, with remorseless blow on blow—
This batterer whom nothing can deter,
Or so he thinks: it is idle of him though—
We are all of us in solitary stir.

II

Our cells are numbered as they should be, planned
For somebody's convenience, and they show
Zip Code, Ess-Ess, Et Cet. Across the land
Call us by phone, or try to. No *Hello!*
Will greet your ears. Ah, Wellaway, ah Woe,
To think that such frustrations can occur!
So, losers-weepers, let the salt tears flow—
We are all of us in solitary stir.

III

Our space is narrow indeed; we stride no strand,
Walk no wide thoroughfare, no Broadway. No,
This cramps our style to something less than grand:
No mountain peaks, no jungles, all plateau,

Barren and bleak, or desolation. Oh
And something else, more grim and crueller:
Cellmates do not exist in Murderer's Row—
We are all of us in solitary stir.

    L'envoi
Villon, file papers for us, with Rimbaud
As witness. Plead the Royal Pardoner
In an appeal; to be denied, we know—
We are all of us in solitary stir.

THE SONNET

We are all of us in solitary stir—
Both adjective and noun advisedly
Employed: the cant of criminals would be
Unworthy in this context. If we err,
Are solecism-prone, with blot and blur
Deface the page, forbid felicity,
Never shall it be said that such as we
Abandoned hope, complaisant to concur.

Under surveillance of our warden's gaze
(I don't mean God at all)—until we die
We take our turns, walk our permitted ways,
Flagstone or gravelled path: reprieve and pardon
Much less to hope for than a hint of sky,
Or momentary glimpse—perhaps—of garden.

SESTINA

Is the finch a widow? Are the lambs in bush?
The weasels warlocks? Silly questions. Hush!—
It lightens—flash and rumble, interval
And then renewal, wind-and-weather blown
There, across Susquehanna: hear the call
Of the night-mail's mellifluous whistle-tone,

Of whose import, most fugitive, we cry
"Is any one aware?" No answers call
There from that country where all wenches die,
The sea-marge, where the kites and kestrels hover
And cormorants wheel above a sunken wall—
It was a causeway once; its day is over.

It (not that sarn, but all the past) we find
Of rack and ruin made, of doggerel rhyme
And *room, dune, doom, rune,* keeping idiot time.
Is the winch winding in this winter wind?
The weasels keep their covens in the caves
There, where among the sepulchers and graves

There is no bringing of the lambs to fold,
It seems, no Perdita attends the shearing.
The simple village life of High Endeavor,
Of church and chapel, dwindles, disappearing.
Is vanishing, is lost, for ever and ever,
And Dick, the shepherd, blows his nail i' the cold.

And now the singers and the dancers, all
There still may be; each, in his hardihood,
Is lacing on the golden shoes. The call
It must be, summons music in the wood
Of *mezzo del camin'*. The leader's raising
The baton for that canticle of praising.

The music swells, and dwells, and dies away,
And the great ship comes to her mooring, Bay
Of Last Resort. The mariners descend
There, and disperse, all up and down the coast.
It takes no more than a few hours at most.
Is anybody left? No, that's the end.

"Is anybody there?" the traveler cried.
It brought no answer, and the echo died
There in the disenchantment of his pride.

VILLANELLE: CALIBAN'S SONG

Be not afeard: the isle is full of noises,
Sounds and sweet innocent airs
That give delight, and hurt not, music, voices

Wherein the heart takes comfort and rejoices,
Even your monster dares
Be not afeard; the isle is full of noises

That, heard in sleep, sing slumber, dreaming's praises,
A long farewell to cares.
Oh, give delight, and hurt not, music, voices

Too beautiful to choose from, with the choices
For eyes as well as ears.
Be not afeard: the isle is full of noises

Bringing richness down from cloud, pictures and phrases
Most seemly in those pairs
That give delight and hurt not, music, voices.

    Far or near, they call across the spaces
    Between our land and theirs.
    Be not afeard: the isle is full of noises
    That give delight, and hurt not. Music. Voices.

WATER COURSE—I

A Song for Lunèd, Lady of the Fountain
(for Lennett Atkinson)

Now let me sing
O my son, O my daughter,
A bright brave thing
Shining, rising
Ice-translucent, clear silver
Its fall, its return
In dew on the fern.

O listeners all,
Miracle-marvelers,
Here there stirs
In the rise and the fall
Music beyond the ear—
For the eyes as well—
Beautiful, lovely
In all of its moving.

From ripple and rill
To the ocean deep
The song might still
Flood, pour, spill;

But this will keep
For a longer story.
Meanwhile, all glory
Sing for the water.

Benedicite,
  Benedicite.

WATER COURSE–II
The Current

After the blessing *Benedicite*,
Listen for infinitesimal whisper, sigh
Of dismissal, of farewell. *Ah well-away*,
Ah well-away! Syntax obscure—
Adverb, verb, interjection? Little difference,
Let's say it's all of them.

                The water seeps,
Curls, around the fern roots, golden, silver,
Royal, Southern Sword; keeps going, widens
To where the farmboy needs a running start
To make the leap across—but little harm
If he falls short, a comic episode
Of soft-loam slip-slide. Downstream, not much farther,
The same boy thinks "About deep and wide enough
To catch a trout in, anyway a small one."
And before long he'll have a swimming pool
In dappled shade, or in an open meadow
With thistle, burdock, mullein, milkweed, daisies.

By now the creeks are rivers, with bridges and names:
Pequest, Musconetcong—they are little streams
Scarcely fifty miles from source to mouth,
Where they slide into those greater rivers,

The ones that carry steamers in their flood,
The Delaware, Hudson, or Susquehanna,
Toward the great bays with the ocean-going vessels,
Out to the deep.

Our atoms veer now, swerve. We are in Thames water
West of London, the only motion a shimmer
As the tide poises, bank-brim-full, for the turn.
There's a barge, moonlight illumined, and strings and flutes
Playing soft and low the music of Handel,
Before the tide turns.

Now the river slides
East, east, through London pool, west into the Channel,
Beyond Land's End, north of the Azores, daring
Windy Twenties, Dirty Thirties, Roaring Forties,
North of the calm Bermoothes, till at last
The wave beats on our stern and rockbound coast.

America! "Oh brave new world, that has
Such people in it!"

A LILT FOR NUNNEY

Nunney town has a castle and moat
Certainly less ostentatious
Than Harlech or Warkworth, but kindly note—
Why, gracious goodness gracious,
You can't win 'em all—no one has yet,
Even in merry, merry Somerset.
Sing—or skip—derry-down-derry.

Somebody painted St. George on the wall,
With a foam-white hart behind him.
It wasn't really a hart at all
But a unicorn come to remind him.
Looking over his shoulder, his shoulder,
Looking over his shoulder.

When there's a unicorn anywhere near
There certainly will be found
Virgins, plenty of virgins, my dear,
With a leap and a skip and a bound.
Virgins, virgins, virgins, virgins,
Searching for maypoles, not for surgeons,
Risqué, frisky, raunchy, randy,
Riddle me, riddle-me-ree.

The font is oval, Norman, and chaste
But what are the vicar and verger doing?
Such antics! Such a scandalous taste,
The liquorous, lecherous pair pursuing,
Belfry to vestry, nuns, nuns, nuns,
One at a time, or a dozen at once
Everywhere through the cloister.
Too many voles in the vestry,
Too few pearls in the oyster.

But don't think Nunney is never staid
Or always a hotbed of harlequins only
Or a good man of business need feel afraid
Of being forlorn and lonely.
No, no—he could do very well in trade,
In a normal year he would find he made
More than a little money.
So, Hey-Nonny-Nonny for Nunney!

LITTLE SONG FOR THE LEAVES
(for Robert Kelley)

Weave, weave the music of the leaves
So that it moves
Our listenings, our loves.
Stir, ever so gently, the rustle of the breeze
In the old trees,
Beech, maple, ash, elm, oak—
Tell over the soft idiom they spoke
To still, to quiet air;
And when they go,
Follow, follow
Follow, fare, whisper them fair
Wherever they are.

CYMRIC PLACES

Here is a wooded slope, where old trees grow—
Hazel and oak, and the red-berried rowan—
Around an island in the nearby hollow
Whose name is "Hollow of the Crooked Furrow."
(What was the matter? Was the ploughman drunk?
No, sober; but sunk in a sorrow.)

Inland fields over whose rye, oats, wheat,
Wind shimmers, ripples, sunshine-sharp-and-sweet;
Under the orchard-green, look up at the fruit—
Orange, gold, red, the faintest hint of white
At stem end, or plum's solid purple, dark
As an omen, mark-rune of the night.

And the gullbreast-soft, smooth-grey lift of the ocean
Brims but breaks not; Rhondda, sleek-oil-slow
Seep-sidles, a sleek slider, black of hue;
While other rivers, three, commingle, flow
In comity together; a cataract's splash
Is a joyful dash of wild motion.

The daily sound is by no means unknown;
There's an anvil and a smithy on one lawn,
Buyers and sellers strolling up and down
At a market fair; in Glendower's court of stone
High deliberations under way
Occupy the day from dusk to dawn.

The beasts are wary: the greyhound has a lair
Trench-deep, above whose parapet he'll peer
Sentinel-wise at intervals; the deer
Makes thicket into lookout; magpie, stare,
Signal each other, flap-wing; chatter in code,
"The end of the road for the Queen draws near."

So, all is woven into wonderment:
The sad, the gay, sinister, innocent,
Surface and substance, marvelously blent;
The Great Hall, trophy-hung; the tinier tent
Brave-bright with pennons flying from its height,
Witness of the light, and testament.

FRISBEE

Flanged, all bright colors—red, yellow, blue, green—discs
Wheel their parabolas, whirl in ellipse,
Soar, dip, or veer—elusive, elegant.
As for the hand that meets them on their way
It's as intended, directing from the shoulder
Patterns of interception, all its length—
Forearm, wrist, hand, and fingers, all indeed
As delicate, fine of grain, not gross of bone—
Precision instrument, supple, adroit, expert.
It makes the outfielder who gets the ball
Out by the warning track a blatant lout,
A clumsy oaf: the fruitpicker who reaches
Tiptoe on ladder-rung for the highest peach,
Apple, or apricot, on the topmost bough,
Cradling it gently, carefully to basket,
Is a lubberly lummox by comparison
With this deft grace, this ease, this perfect neatness.
There are such scenes on Cretan mixing bowls,
On amphoras, on jars for honey, for oil:
Young men and maidens, marvelous in skill,
Leaping on bulls or horses, as John Keats
Saw and remembered—the shared attitude,
With brede of marble men and maidens wrought
To exquisite perfection, poised or moving.

Oh, never play this game with ugly clothes on.

THE QUEST

Valor and Probity no longer dwell
Within our city, but are faring far
Down roads of dark, whereof no guidebooks tell,

Pathways illumined by no glint of star.
It drizzles a cold rainfall. Marble hail
Bounces, and sleet drives pelting. And there are

No jolly rollickers along this trail
Caroling antic music, never sung
In this depressed and smog-infected vale.

From barren trees, or blighted ones, are hung
Festoons like parasitic Spanish moss—
Except that these are ordure, reeking dung

From beasts, or men, or demons, all across
That valley of desolation. This I know
From hearsay, or experience. Gain or loss,

Who can be sure? I hear a summons: *Go
And bring them back*, they order me. "But why
May I not first seek someone's help? This foe

Is pitiless, a monster. What can I
Do by myself against his carrion rage?"
The answer came in one word only—*Try*.

But no man could be found, no man my age
To second me, as fellow challenger;
No stripling volunteered as squire or page.

Only one creature made the slightest stir
Toward me—not eagle, lion, man, nor ox,
But just a mangy little pup, a cur

Much like hyena, jackal, slyboot fox,
Or something braver, rushing out to me
Like a fierce gopher from his lair of rocks,

All ardor and fire, except for times when he
Was scared: some seven days in every week
Would be about his quota; I could see

No other stigma of a yellow streak
In my adoring Cerberus-watcher, so
Affectionate, so intense. I called him Zeke.

Of course, we should have started long ago
But there was something first. I knew that I
Must have some sign, some mark, from which to know

Our quarry's essences, identify
Their ways, to make them clear beyond all doubt.
Valor would carry a sword, but Probity?

Would he go with all his pockets inside out
To prove he was not venal? If he took
A secret ring, or stone, how could he flout

His candor, justify disguise? But look,
We gave ourselves the proper answer when
We said "His life was like an open book."

44

The weather worsens. Clouds writhe into men
Who strike and vanish in the slash of sleet,
And men are boulders and dissolve again

Into a mucus-broth around our feet,
Pus-colored, viscid, hardening like glue,
A quagmire-suction, rotting moss and peat.

We must have traveled faster than we knew,
For suddenly there were two of them, who stood
Halving the road, and it was surely true

One had a sword; and each one wore a hood
And mask, one red, one black. We did not see
Anyone with a book in hand. How could

We at that distance? But as soon as we
Came closer, yes, one had a book; he tore
Its pages out, and ripped them viciously.

This, for some reason, gave us heart. The more
We looked, the more we hoped for. All in vain—
A children's book of comics. What a bore!

As for the sword, it proved to be a cane
Such as old gaffers use for prop and stay,
Not even blackthorn. What was there to gain

From such cheap stuff? We must be on our way,
I thought, and suited action to the word.
What absolute and utter folly lay

In that decision! What morosis blurred
My omadhaun wit! How could I be so dense?
Too late, too late, before I saw and heard.

Even Dr. Watson would have had the sense
To see through such diaphanous disguise,
Unriddle clues, with sound intelligence.

Not I. In going on I heard their cries,
"After him, after him!" and the pursuit
Came on, implacable. Hope fades and dies,

Driven by such relentless, resolute
Onset; and I, confronted by a wall
Too strong to break, too high to overshoot,

Turned, as I had to turn, and summoned all
My resolution, every bit of nerve
That I possessed, faced them, tried not to fall,

Did what I could to stand erect, not swerve,
Not faint, not die. I had no other choice
But use my last consignment of reserve,

And saw a hand reach out, and heard a voice
Calling to me, most musical and mild,
"Be comforted; be happy, and rejoice;

We knew we should go back, but, oh, dear child,
We needed you so much. Now nothing bars
Your being with us." As he spoke, they smiled,

And their eyes held a shining like the stars.

46

DIALOGUE

"What wonderful weather!"
"But the windflowers wither."

"The dancers are lively."
"Their leaps are not lovely
And their lips are uncomely."

"How green is my valley . . ."
"Where sharpshooters volley
And Bashan bulls bellow."

"I do enjoy the wildflowers in the meadow."
"Poor things! below that ominous cloud shadow,
The rain and hail will pelt them silly."

"How marvelous the magic of the hazel!
How pure—the tone, the music, of the minstrel."
"The nut tree roots are gnawed on by the weasel.
The player hears no murmur of approval."

"Vermilion, royal blue—delightful color!
Golden and silver, every rainbow hue."
"They fade, you know; they become gray, or duller,
Lose even an ashen glow."

"Aromas? Jasmine, lilac, spikenard, myrrh?"
"*Merde alors!*"

"Poor wretch! Will nothing ever
Inform your voice to praise?"
"Of course not. Far be any such infection
From all my ways.
Good Lord, deliver
Me from so gross a folly—
From uttering needless noise."

CONTRA NATURAM

Sun, be Joshua: gesture, call
"Halt!" to the days' processional.

King Canute, from the edge of the strand
Beckon the waves to come inland
For a bite to eat, and a sip to sup
In the royal halls. Feed full; drink up!

Jeremiah (né Gloomy Gus),
Couldn't you change with Pandarus—
Your solemn weeds for his archer's breeches—
And goose some Cressida till she screeches?

In the evening-cool descent of the dew
The Lord in the garden calls to you,
Adam, with fond approving voice,
"Be of good cheer, my son, rejoice.
Eating the apple has made you wise
And cost you only a Paradise."

Alfred ("Apeneck") Prufrock grins,
Poses and swirls in the Spanish cape,
Taking a look at the Seven Sins:
The one to start with, he thinks, is rape.
Let no floor-creature start to rise;
It would be premature to reorganize.

"Every third thought" says Prospero
"Will henceforth be my grave," and so
He puts aside his magic book—
To bend, with anxious frowning look
Over his little grandson's crib,
The fallen toys, the messy bib.

"Northward ho!" cries Ahab. "Set all sail—
What's Moby Dick but just another whale?"

What does all this prove, except that men
Once in a blue moon, now and then,
Tire of the daily round, would change
The too-familiar for the strange?
Don't worry; they'll all come home again.

COAT ON A STICK

"Coat on a stick, coat on a stick!
Why, you old scarecrow, you're making me sick."

"That's all right, Buster; that's quite all right.
I don't give myself any great appetite."

"Clap hands and sing, clap hands and sing!
At your age that's a ridiculous thing."

"Maybe you're right, young man; even so
I might be getting some fun from it, though."

"And this chatter of tatter in mortal dress—
Does the matter have any significance?" "Yes,

My fop days are over, I'm starting to fray,
I'll be stark naked almost any day."

"Well, well. Would you mind stating that in some
Less metaphor-embrangled idiom?"

"All right. You know, of course, that all men die
And before any too long, so must I.

A prospect I'm aware that I must face
With acquiescence, if not perfect grace."

"Poor fellow! No more gyring with the sages,
No stunts and capers round the Rock of Ages?"

"Exactly. Only the intense profound
Absorption of the ash-receiving ground."

THE DEEPENING SHADES

From the rich dark of the leaves, the mockingbird
Still sings; the song is heard
As I turn off the light; the song
Will vary and recur the whole night long.
They are opposing advocates, the dark
And music—learnèd counselors, who plead
With cunning, eloquent rede.
One argument is clear and simple: "Hark,
Listen and hear most delicate sweet airs."
The other answers: "Rest, retire; good rest
Is of all precious balms the loveliest
In medication's anodyne for cares."
Both arguments persuade, almost. My clue
Is given in *The Deepening Shades*. I know
Thereby, which choice to make, which way to go.
My dear, I leave the inference to you.

WITH GARB OF PROOF

"...with garb of proof shield me from out the prease
Of those fierce darts Despair at me doth throw"
—*Sir Philip Sidney*

"With garb of proof"—but where, in our time, find
Armor invisible, chain-mail for the heart
Against all flight of evil, each fierce dart
Tipped with peculiar poison, in a wind
Implacable, incessant, and combined
With sleet-sting, gnat-bite? What surpassing art
Can stop, break, turn, that arrow fire, or part
That cloud of menace-motes around the mind?

Ah, good Sir Philip, as you must have known,
That was no light demand you laid on Sleep
As officer, but I would wish my own
More vigilant, my watch and ward to keep,
Alert, responsible, a sentinel
More open-eyed, to guard, and wish me well.

A SONG FOR MORTIMER

Ah, my beloved
Rest you, repose you
Under the rose-hue
Red-bud of rowan—
Soft be the bed.

My dear, my darling
Music is making
Airs all around
For the sake of your slumber;
Sleep sound, sleep sound.

Then, my great warlord,
Awaken, draw sword.
Rest and repose
Have whetted the blade
To receive the red blood,

Life-wine of our foes—
Spilled crimson, a stain
On the shag of the stone
Or mist-fire, steaming upward
From coign and from courtyard.

"MARY MORSE,
MARY MORSE"

The house is about
Across the street
From the Methodist Church,
And not too far
From the fresh fish store
Of Harry Burch.

"Mary Morse, Mary Morse,
Come in off the porch!
It is Saturday night
And the drunken men
Are simply reeling."

Spoken with feeling
And good sound sense,
No fake compassion
For boozy gents
Who stagger, lurch,
Get up, fall down,
On their way down town.

In the Tidd House bar
Or the Ochs Hotel
The prices are,
Say, suitable,
Though the quality
Not what good rye
Should really be.

"Mary Morse, Mary Morse"—
A girl, fourteen,
In a summer dress,
On a summer night,
Is a lovely sight.

But she might arouse
Much viciousness
In some red-eyed souse.
"Mary Morse, Mary Morse,
Come into the house."

TO HIS MISTRESS,
MARVELLOUSLY FROWARD

"Had we but world enough"—but, Lady,
We've much too much damn world already.
Humber and Ganges roll their floods
Past over-teeming multitudes;
A vegetable love would be
More fitting for humanity.
If it takes nothing but the pill
T'inspire thy willing soul to will—
Lady, forget it; keep thy cool
And do not be a god damn fool.

Rather, let chastity combine
The dust and ashes, yours and mine,
So that I hear, behind my back
No scythe-outfitted hearse or hack.
Let your quaint honor do its best
To keep on being quaint; the rest
We leave to Fortune, with a sense
Of rather modest continence.
Thus, though we cannot make our son
Exist, we do know how 'tis done.

BAILIWICK

(Fantasia in E-sharp major,
or Six No Diamonds)

A bailiwick is like a borough
Where boundaries, perhaps, are narrow
But also absolutely thorough,
Lasting beyond the last tomorrow,
Beyond all works of art by Corot
Or pencils made by H. D. Thoreau.
No ploughshare drives a lustral furrow
More definite than this; no harrow
Can pulverize the lines to zero.
Where Queen Anne's Lace grows wild, and yarrow
Is rank, conducive to our sorrow,
Expect no brave romantic hero
Trained in the colleges of Cairo,
Or maybe Rio de Janeiro,
Or even faraway Fort Barrow,
To come, supplied with bow and arrow
By some absurd insistent bureau
As proper weapons for a tyro
To use against a tyrant Pharaoh,
To massacre a sow with farrow
Of eighty pigs, or shoot a sparrow.
Dressed in serape and sombrero,

Musicians, loathing to their marrow
What they play next, Ravel's *Bolero*,
Tune up their fiddles, much like Nero,
Before the last chiaroscuro.

Hergest's Red Book is said to be
Our most profound authority
On early Cymric poetry.
It tells us that the passage here
Breaks off, is nothing but a mere
Fragment, whose fuller scope confines
Its bulk to some eight hundred lines
All based, of course, on the same rhyme,
But no surprise, to meet with some
Proest variation in the scheme.

People who know Welsh bardcraft well
Think this is highly plausible.

Next we behold Chief Justice Bayard
Whose antics have us running scared;
Almost as if nobody cared
When deans went on debauches, dared
Find fault with Philomel, and fared
To where licentious lions laired
Or predatory panthers paired
Before the hunters got them snared.
Too proud to spit or snarl, they aired
Their grievances by saying *Mairde—*
How delicately French!—and squared
Their consciences with unimpaired
Conviction that their course was shared
By many lovely golden-haired
Lassies at whom the lustful stared
In lewd libido, and despaired.
What cause, what case, could be compared
To theirs, at whom the darkness bared
Volpine fangs, at whom there blared
Flatulent buglers, unprepared
To play their music while they glared.
More trash the reader should be spared,
Therefore, as ordered, so declared.

AS COMPARED WITH
THE ESKIMOS

Dancing around our maypoles, go
Every slob, schlemiel, and schmo.
Now would you not suppose they might
Just now and then get something right?
Don't kid yourself, my friend. They claim
A more exclusive hold on Fame,
Whose incorruptible silence (James)
Rejects, along with other claims,
This one of theirs, says "No, no, no!"
To every slob, schlemiel, and schmo.
What can they do but dance around
In futile folly, being bound
To their supreme ineptitude,
Conspicuous, and crass, and crude?
America! God shed His grace
On Pottsville, Pottstown, Peyton Place,
As long as from our sluices flow
Every slob, schlemiel, and schmo.

CAMANO ISLAND
(for Beth Bentley)

I

No one in sight along this island shore
This warm and windless early afternoon;
We'll not hear people, either, very soon.
But one lone bird contrives to sound like more,
At least a hundred of his kind, a loon,
Or duck, or blend of both, bizarrely bred
By *Gavia Stellata*, via scaup
Or scoter egg—not only turtles tread—
Hear his barbaric yawp!

II

Not really yawp, though; more like a giggle, or string
Of giggles in quick sequence—*bleep, bleep, bleep, bleep,*
    bleep—
All dots, no dashes, cacchination's ghost
Singing (or so it thinks) itself to sleep,
A giggle's echo, on that lonely coast,
In dark and vain regret,
"Close folded now is every weary wing"—
I wonder what acoustics you would get
Playing it backward on your recording set?

III

That day, along that shore, no cockle-shells
Were turned to silver bells, but we did find
Plenty of urchins and mussels, which by now
Like agates, we have far too many of
In our home treasures, and we always vow
Never again! But just the same, in love
We bring them back, whose efficacy dwells
Within us, warmth of body and mind
Against mean winter's witch-and-wizard spells.

OF REDOLENCE

(for Bill Coles)

I

Not by the sights do we recall this town,
The arching trees, maple and elm and oak,
Not by town common, or the college halls
Red and white Georgian, built by farmer folk
Who valued learning, valued piety,
Invited cap and gown
To train their sons in proper decency.
Terras irradient, the motto calls.

II

Nor by the sounds do we remember: bells
Of town and college halls, that never struck
The hour together, though at times they'd come
Almighty close. And not the rush of the brook
Down by the Grist Mill, much too much acclaimed
As "river", but brought low
To a more fitting fluency, and named
The Freshman; really, that was not too dumb.

III

What of the sense of touch? Our hands and fingers
Are less availing than our plantigrade
Exploratory gear; those double bringers
March us from home to where the game is played
On sidewalk, pavement, (Hitchcock Road's the name)
A narrow strip of cinder track,
Green turf, clay infield, crunch of boundary lime,
Up wobbly planks with numbers painted black.

IV

No, not on any of these—although they well
Merit our notice of a lovely place—
Do we rely, but on the sense of smell,
To bring fulfillment, satisfy with grace
Fond recollection, give us back a mood,
Oh, very, very good,
Release, with greatest potency and power,
The concentrated essence of the hour.

V

For instance? —To begin with, very trite,
The smell of burning leaves. Then apples, gold
Or red, almost unbruised, picked up from grass
Which dew still beads; or that more ugly yield,
The brown, squashed, yellow-jacket-teeming mess;
Aroma, resinous, of pine
No more than stirred by breezes in the night;
Grapes, Concord or Niagara, on the vine.

VI

You'll have to help me now, Bill. I suppose
I might, with luck, hit on a thing or two
That made a powerful appeal to you,
But after all my nose is not your nose—
This is about as far as I should go.
O balsam! O bay! O mint! O musk! O myrrh!
I sign off, Bill, as your simpatico
And thoroughly devoted thurifer.

THE WALKER AT DUSK
(for Ted Baird)

Oh, it's superbly beautiful around
This town right now; walking the woods, you find
Light rising like a music from the ground
At dusk; the whole world flowing, in a wind
Of color, not substantial, nearly so—
Wherever you go, attend, respond!

Superbly beautiful—a wonder,
A world whose promise, over and over,
Is light, is music, both together—
A rise, a flow, with wind and color
Combined to make one essence, far and high,
A sweep over sky, a lower stir.

The town indeed is very beautiful
When dusk is light, with music visible
For miles around, and color like a call
To celebrate high mysteries, to dwell
With Helen, join Ulysses bound for home—
Blue-green swell, white foam, the furl of sail.

THE CHILLBLAIN INDIANS

They suffer intensely in such altitude
As ours in Leadville, Georgetown, Silver Plume,
Which they denounce as very far from good,
A soppy, stagnant pampa, drenched in rheum
Below sea level, like a dam or dike
Mitten-thumb-plugged by that heroic tyke,
The little Dutch boy.

                Their Chileño sires
Banked all the hectic ardor of their fires
With daughters of the Plumèd Knight of Maine,
That honorable member, James G. Blaine.

As for the squaws, they are really pretty lax
As cooks, or as mop-wielders. Artifacts
They putter with, carved from the local bones
Of limber lemmings, or from cherry stones,
Or Painless Parker dentures. Their designs
For what they claim are tribal totem poles
Use infinitely tiresome blurry lines.
And on their flutes, which have only two holes,
They record folk songs of their long ago,
Two numbers: *Yes, yes, yes*; and *No, no, no*.

It's easy to contrive, devise, invent
Creatures of such distorted guise as these
Obnoxious Chillblain aborigines,
As obviously fake and flatulent.
By now, I think, you probably agree
With a conviction that has dawned on me,
Or—put it this way—I'll believe with you
No grievous loss of culture would ensue
If never a Chillblain ever came to birth
On this our many-venom'd, over-peopled earth.

LA COUSINE

Winter has its delights. On Sundays, often,
When a spot of sun makes gold the white terrain
You take a stroll with a charming little cousin.
"Don't you be late for dinner!" Mother says.

All right. The Tuileries arbor gives your round
Embedded elegance, green on winter ground.
The young lady's cold. She shivers. And your eyes
Note evening mist beginning to arise.

So, home again. By now it is late and murky.
Sigh with discretion, ardor, and regret
Over bright hours which quickly fade and fail.

Cross the sill to warmth, but do not yet
Ascend the stair; pause briefly and inhale
The full rich redolence of roasting turkey.

ARACHNE, PENELOPE

Arachne, at her loom,
All ready, in the tall and spacious room
High-beamed and groined with oak, saw, out beyond
The window, going to and from the pond,
The blackbird, lustrous, with vermilion arc
On shoulder-wing, illumining his dark,
His more extensive jet. And as he flew
Arachne never knew
Whether his shuttle imitated hers,
Followed her weaving, cut past stave of reed,
Past rest of water in that flash of speed
Which more than stirs
The senses—brightness bountiful!—or whether
This one, or that, was follower. Together
They made the music, the response, the cry
Of contrapuntal color harmony.

And on a far-off isle a queen, for love,
By night unravelled what her patience wove
All the long day. Who helped her? Loneliness
And Solitude. No others came to bless,
To bring angelic sustenance. Alone,
Somewhat beyond her middle way, she stood
Companioned by no presence but her own
In that malignant wilderness and wood.
But she was making music there, such song

As never sounds but out of threnody,
Out of lament, and all its airs belong
To the great hymn we title Victory—
Rejoice, we are winning! News the runner brought
Athens from Marathon is ours to hear
In reverent assembly as we ought,
Making the very silence, grave and clear,
Cry with exultant voice
We win; rejoice, rejoice.

WESTWARD HO!

From those ancient city walls
Sometimes known as Bellows Falls
Via Brattleboro, bound
For the sights of Puget Sound,
Bainbridge Island, Bremerton,
In the occidental sun,
Men go faring, blithe and gay,
Westward Ho! along their way.

Far from Quoddy's icy gales
On to Gambell, on to Wales,
No rude jostling, no mad rush
Through the suburbs of La Push,
Lemming imitators wend
Till they reach their journey's end
Even beyond Chichagof.
Who will scorn? Who dares to scoff?

League on league, unquitted quest
Out past Kiska, from Key West
Toward the rage of that wild shore
Whose reverberations roar.
Turbulence, confusion, pound
In combative shock of sound,
In the elemental brawling,
Sea-wind rising, storm-rain falling.

Only possibly, there will
Come a moment, calm and still,
Like the center of the eye
When the hurricane goes by,
When the rampant reel and riot
Decently subside to quiet
And we hear at last the long
Silence, blesseder than song.

THE BETTER THEME

Music of goldfinch-flight across a corner of upland,
Scarlet tanager in mulberry tree,
Red fox on stone wall, proclaiming his lordship,
Utter stillness at night—how can there be
Deeper music than this, or changes played
More happily on the theme? Let the hatred go
Where it belongs, to the sidehill junk-yard; rust,
Crumble, pit, pock, flake, fuse with all ugliness
In nothing, nothing at all, the domain of dust.

Return, come back again from *No* to *Yes*,
To oriole color, vireo warble, bright
Sleek-pouring millpond flow
Out of still waters. Stop, look, listen. Know
One sound, itself all music: in the night
The whistle of the train, far, far away
From where we lie and listen in the dark,
Rousing enough to say
"There's the Black Diamond. Hark!"

Here is our state of grace. Oh, brave new world
That has such wonders in it! Come not nigh
Our province, all ye monsters of the sky,
Ocean, and earth; but let fair comeliness
With good persuasion bless
The lot of our possessing, courtesy
Attend our walks abroad, and finally,
Rejoice in sharing with our guest-friend Love
The household air, wherein we breathe and move.

SAID BY THE MAN
WHO WOULD BE WELL

I

The stir, the fermentation
On Massa's old plantation
Were almost our salvation,
But met that combination
Rule of Three, Rule of Thumb,
Which certainly have come
Oh, most auspiciously,
In synergic embrace
For the health of the race.

II

The pearl in the oyster,
The verger (non-virgin)
Beginning to roister
In an apse of the cloister
Where the monkshood-buds burgeon,
The lark on the wing
And the snail on the thorn
Lift their voices, and sing
"Better not to be born."

III

But these are the cynics,
So pay them no heed,
Kick them out of the clinics
Where maladies breed
Dispel them with speed,
Oh, give them the air,
And welcome the hearty
Rejoicers, the fair,
The lives of the party.

IV

A bang or a whimper?
Don't stand there and simper!
I vote for a bang,
For the chorus that rang
When the morning stars sang,
The lugubrious lost,
The horror-bound host
Gone, like a ghost
To the mansion of dust.

THE CEDAR WAXWING

In plumage smooth as any velvet cassock
The vain rich novice wears,
All costliness, all gracious airs,
The bird's coat is a lustrous brown, some bright
Tiny red gouts across its dark, a sign
Of candle-drip, wound, blood; the base
Is marked off by a crosswise yellow line.

This bird is not an angel; mask and hood
Of black portend no good,
And what about that crest?
Does it rear up to say
"Every thing we look upon is blest"?
Does it proclaim, suggest
Gloria, *Laus Deo*, *Benedicite*?

Now all that value, valor, virtue, all, all, all
Fallen.

FINALE

What lights, looming, out of sunken sarn
In the gray-ghost haze, in the mist-morn?
A coach with four black horses, born
Sons of apocalypse, breathing scorn
On the weird world they watch, every wretch,
All agony, each retch, twist, and turn.

But brightness might be burning bush, thorn,
All thicket fire, wonderful warning—
No grim grieving, and let no man mourn,
Be tempest-trouble-tossed, taken, torn
By the wide wind, whirling over moor,
Sea-element, sure to scald and burn.

Rising in air intensely, thrush-song
Cries deep sorrow in its native tongue
And says in Welsh "Hiraeth" for longing
While the wild wind wails "Hwyl," high and strong
In passionate call to sea and sky
Fierce in its outcry, bell-peal, bronze-clang.

And all that water does, the bright rush,
River-smooth to sea-arm, cascade crash
Over bedrock base, spray and splash
And spume, far-flung, in frolic and flash,
Abounding, all merriment, in gay air
To happy heights where the breeze blows fresh.

What more? A host, almost past the shores
Of life, the atomic dancing pours
Effulgent rainfall, light-fall, fires
More than million times a million, stars
In infinite number. Pause, bestow
Growth upon us, oh eternal powers!

TRANSCENDENCE

The stars of morning sang
Their great exultant harmony, which rang,
Filled every void along the shores of light,
Deep bass, high treble, blent
To be each one the other's complement,
Splendor celestial, glorious and bright.

By nones, the volume of the bass has thinned,
Rising not quite so high above the ground,
Diminuendo, subsidence, more wind
Than gale by now, a gentler stir
In lower atmosphere;
At vespers, nowhere to be sensed or found.

And higher, higher, higher,
Up to the limits of the ethereal fire,
With passionate intensity, the air,
The treble, rises, melody, all pure,
In whose full range of tone
There is no other nature than its own.

Sundown. Afterglow. Dusk, not quite dark.
Music, descending, dwindles. Hark!
A lovely voice, not too familiar, heard
In the song of a single bird,
The hermit thrush, whose perfect air
Is liquid-clear, water distilled from fire.

"The water-dripping song," even so
The books described it, many years ago.

FIVE FINGER EXERCISE

Albemarle Beach contains
   The usual designs
   Spotted in all marines.

Dune, ebb, flow—
   Sand and tides come and go.

Ground-swell heaving in jetty-jut
   Near where pier-piles, barnacle-pitted, rot.

Kelp—
   Where Scylla's blue-groined sea dogs yelp.

Low mist, never ocean's proud quarrelsome rage—
   Leo asleep, and snoring in his cage.

Strong tidal undertow—
   Sand and tides come and go.

Violent wave-wrack—
   Over, and out, and back.

Xerox your zest—
   Then—relax! Rest!

A GENTLE THING

Sleep's room is dark; its portals loose his care,
His luminous courtesy, across the air
To soothe men's fret and fume, abate despair,

By the due warrant of his office, give,
Majestic in his pure prerogative,
The double benefice whereby we live,

His ruse, which keeps the greatest of his kin
A prisoner, enfolded deep within
The halls of dark, his murderer, his twin,

His drowsing brother, on and over whom
The investiture, the habiliments of doom,
Weigh heavy, oppress, in that rich luxurious room.

His rune, whose virtue is the healing spell,
The potent charm against the powers of Hell,
Is exhortation, "Oh, be well, be well!

Prosper, be tall in all abundance, grow
In grace, and come all in good time to know
Each third grave thought, as wise as Prospero."

THE SCREAMING MEEMIES

The Screaming Meemies is a term
For one of man's worst diseases.
But how does he catch it? From a germ?
A virus? Insufficient sperm?
Nobody knows, by Jesus.

What does the patient do, undone
By this infection? Must it run
On a fixed course, or can it be
Reversible? Its pathology
Is marked by what stigmata? Clot,
Bleb, canker, cyst? Or is there not
One plainer sign, whereby to trace
The morbid aspects of each case?

Well, let's see what he does: he jumps
High as he can; does grinds and bumps;
Sings dirty songs off-key; and whistles
Hymns from his church's latest missals;
He makes himself extremely nervous
By memorizing Poems of Service.

Fatigue sets in at last; he crawls
Back through a cranny in the walls
To spend the remnant of his night
In most unedifying fright.
"Have mercy on him, Lord!", we pray,
By Ember Day he'll be o. k.

THE BOURGEOIS

So, in they come and make their way
For a most casual survey
Where all the masterpieces mark
Man's triumphs out of inner dark.
Does this impress them? Not a mite,
They're anesthetic to delight.
What does this get us but abuse?
Let's turn these fatuous fellows loose,
Enjoining them to cease to roister
But go hunt up the nearest cloister,
Find cell door Number 33,
Inviting them to turn the key.
They do so, and in consequence
Wander down avenues of tents,
For leagues and leagues, until the shore
Darkens with breakers—roll, rush, roar—
And all dissolves in chaos, all
Swirls to that state before the fall,
And anarchs reign, and angels die
In rubble, trash, and junk of sky.

TO DREAD, TO WELCOME

Crash and reverberation of night thunder;
Faint light at dawn; a stir of air; the slender
Sanderling skitterers squeak above their plunder—
They are finders all, who never wait nor wonder.
By noon the tide's at flood, and ocean's boom
Havoc-loud is loom, is cloud-reminder.

Peace be with you! Look inland, where the maple,
Scarlet in September, near the steeple
Of College Hall, is bright—red, yellow apple,
Wealthy, Delicious, whose appeal to people
Is flavor, odor, almost touch and cry;
And the crushed ones lie, late jug-tipple.

Hurricane! Leaves on ground, trees bent over,
Implacable sound, its roar crescendo, ever
To full sick-shock, dumbfoundedness and fever,
Din, dreadful, pinion-thrash, and harpy-hover,
Harpy-descent, and dive, and harpy-stench,
The fouling of branch, loose-noise lover.

"Still waters, no moving!" So the children's order,
Their mild injunction, their beginning ardor
For the game Run-a-Mile, was guide, was guarder,
While moonlight, luminous at bound and border,
Poured forth such a flood, rush of the rain,
Continual gain, no friend fonder.

And Fire, the absolute Devastator,
Arch abolitionist, Ash-and-Dust Creator,
Merciless Moloch, heartless Immolater,
Whose anger snarls and crackles, worse than bitter,
Whose dry-mouthed hunger gluts itself and feeds
Even on seaweeds, horror, hater.

Almost beyond the ways of atmosphere
The love-drawn stars are moving, bright and clear;
So far away their presence, they appear
A cloud at rest, held in the dazzling air—
Vision and verity, quiet in space,
Quick with life, with grace. How brave! How dear!

ADAGE, TRIAD

A doctor a day
Keeps the apple away:
Gravenstein, Spy,
Russet or Greening.
There are three ills
Nobody wills:
Bedsores and bills,
Words without meaning.

A pig in a poke
Is a juvenile joke:
A fraud and a freak
Not even funny.
Three are the powers
Each man desires:
Muscles like Mars,
Mad mirth, more money.

Nine stitches are
Nothing to fear
In repair of a scar
From falling, or fight.
Three lovely sounds
Are: bells, and the wind's
Laughter at lands,
Train-whistles at night.

"Sour grapes!" But suppose
Somebody knows
Such riches as those
Are ready to eat.
There are three dowers
For delight of our dears'
Deepest desires:
Silk, diamonds, plate.

The mood of the moss
Craves no caress
As the stone rolls across
Its comforting level.
Three things repel
The hateful in Hell:
Penance, good will,
Holy Water the Devil.

One could go on
Till every last one
Of the proverbs was done
Finally placed.
Three simple queries
Halt your vagaries:
"Why?", "Who wants worries?"
"Have you no taste?"

Don't count your chicks
With premature looks
Or you'll be in a fix
Past all believing.
Three are the joys
For ultimate choice:
Laughter and praise,
Rapture in living.

BEOWULF COUNTRY

They wake, they sleep
In a land ill known,
Wolf packs, wind-sweep
Bleached with bone
Perilous paths
Past the foot of swaths,
Windows, of stone.

Around quagmires,
Mist-steamy moors
To a tarn, deep, deep,
Deep-brown and dark
And not too far
A mountain torrent,
A noisome current
Where evils are
And assassins lurk,
Black hoods in the murk.

Count it in time
Or measured miles,
It's no great climb
To the Lake of Trolls
Trees, hoar-frost white
Cast a blood-stopping light,
Menacing, frowning
Intensely down.

One can say this spot
(With no loss of face),
Is most certainly not
A pleasant place.

IDENTITY CRISIS

*"It will be success if I have
left myself behind."*
— *Thoreau*

What did he go to the woods to see?
The sight of his lost identity?
No, sir! He went there to look at a tree.

Did he see one, or only his beautiful soul
Restored to him perfectly sane and whole?
He saw a tree, the bough and the bole,

The blossom, the cone, needle, tassel, the rest
Where the little red hawks constructed a nest
That high, that near the top of the crest.

Went ye out for to see a prophet? Yes, more,
A man who looked long at a tree, before
Eying that idol too many adore,

The wonderful self, whom he scorned, as he should
As all very well, but not very much good
Compared with a tree standing tall in a wood.

THE GREEN LAND-FALL

The beautiful, smooth, green, even fall
Downhill from the stone of the War Memorial
Comes, widening still, still green, still smooth, descending
To the margin of its ending
In deep left field. With blankets and with beer
The boys and girls make rocks, make islands here
Or what might look like them, except they have
No ruggedness, no splash of wave,
Around them curl no breakers, and they show
No visible glimpse that they do move or flow.

Incidents? One I vividly recall—
The time John Warnock hit that long fly ball,
So deep the runner tagged, came all the way
To score the run. What an amazing play!

Mostly, though, what I would and do preserve
In memory, are the graciousness, the curve,
The texture almost felt, the color seen
In the full richness of its emerald green,
The way all motes and all the elements
Combine to reaffirm the total sense,
The harmony, the cadences that flow,
With sound the essential substance as they go.
How simple! Yet where else in all my days
Have I found side-hill half as worth my praise?

WHO HATH SEEN?
(for Constance Carrier)

Wind, moulder of sand and snow,
Dune shape, dune light, dune shadow.

Contour-maker, whose talent
Is intuitive, intent

On seeing, under the less
Veil coverings of darkness

The scripture, deeply graven,
Too deep for the eyes of man.

Clean, live wind, supreme artist,
Exposing the faux-pas of mist.

NOTES

11. The Beardmanica owes his existence in the first place to Kit Smart; in the second, to Ron Gordon, who used Smart's lines as part of his dedication to me of the Honors Thesis in English which was done under my supervision at Amherst College in 1965.

13. Morning, Old Style came out of a test-question in my Amherst Creative Writing Course. I set the class a prose passage, asking them to locate in it the nucleus of a poem, and to write a few sample lines. As often, I became intrigued by my own question, and worked out an answer; in this particular effort, I found the key cadence in the last two lines here, which set the tone and the rhythm. A good deal of the detail was not in the original prose.

15. Fugue for the Vernal Equinox. The first two lines of the poem are quoted from a letter sent me by Porter Dickinson, reference librarian in the Robert Frost Library at Amherst College. I have used what the Welsh call *proest* rhyming: we say "off-" or "slant" rhyme.

16. Ballade of Wolfville. Written *ad hoc* as lead for an article about Alfred Henry Lewis (1855–1914), author of many tales of Wolfville and of other books. My article appeared in *The Nation*, and as introduction to *Wolfville Yarns* (1968).

18. Belmont is a poem whose theme I have had in mind for at least twenty years. It was not done *ad hoc* for the reopening of Belmont Park this year, though that was a catalytic factor. Let me add that all the racing colors mentioned in the last section are real; and all the horses are real, except two: Right Royal and Red Ember, who are in John Masefield's steeplechase poem, "Right Royal." All the horses save one were also winners—the French horse, Epinard, ran second to Wise Counsellor, Ladkin, and Sarazen. I named one of these horses Co-Educator, by Campus Fusser—Teddy Martin.

22. *Silence, Godhead.* Since 1947, as the poem states, I had the silence passage in mind; but it lacked completion. This was supplied by Epicurus, Lucretius, and useful notes to my translation of Lucretius by George Strodach, Head of the Philosophy Department at Lafayette College.

24. *The Spear Not Broken.* Wallace Stegner's *All the Little Live Things* induced some speculation about the role of the "square," and this involved questions as to who was, and who wasn't. The title comes from Chesterton's eulogy of Bernard Shaw in his book on GBS.

26. *Success Story* has no basis in fact except that one can major in mountaineering at the University of Colorado, and that such majors in the summer time look like the footballers in the fall—with crutches, assorted bandages, etc.

28. *Ballade and Sonnet.* Both, using the same theme, stick close to the demands of the form, but there is an attempt at a more high-power implication.

30. *Sestina.* Here the form has been modified by removing the required end-words to the beginnings of lines and making them as unobtrusive as possible (even so, they have something to say about the meaning). To off-set this lack of color, rhyme has been brought in at line-ends.

32. *Villanelle: Caliban's Song.* This also varies the form by shortening the middle line, and using some slant rhyme. And how wonderful of Shakespeare to give the monster Caliban some of the loveliest lines in the play!

33. *Water Course.* Part I, *A Song for Lunèd.* Lunèd is a lady of Welsh legend; her name is cognate with Lynette's, but she is not as saccharine a creature as the one in Tennyson's *Idylls.* Part II is mostly self-explanatory except for the irrational "atomic swerve" from daytime on the Delaware, Hudson, Susquehanna, to dark on the Thames.

37. *A Lilt for Nunney.* My grandfather, Henry Humphries, may have been born in this town in Somerset, and certainly went to school there; my sister has his exercise books in elementary math. The properties, moat, castle, font, mentioned in the poem, are authentic; the people and their antics, my invention.

39. *Little Song for the Leaves.* This recalls the few moments before the horses come to saddling enclosures or the walking ring—or elsewhere, some other time and place. This short

poem owes its existence to Bob Kelley, who wrote *Time Magazine* in praise of my "Belmont" poem: "stirring the breeze of memory so that it moves a few lovely leaves on the old trees."

40. Cymric Places. This poem was designed around a series of Welsh place names, whose translation suggests the various stanzas. The meter—*hir a thodaidd*—is one of my favorites among the twenty-four officially recognized by the schools of the bards.

42. Frisbee. Another poem which I wanted to write for a long time before I eventually got around to it. This originally appeared in the *New Yorker*, but was revised in January, 1969.

43. The Quest. It is Dante's *terza rima*, of course, as to form; more irrational—not exactly surrealist—in treatment of the theme: confusion of good and evil, pursuer and pursued; courage and wit turning to cowardice and folly. In the end, the point Louise Bogan made in *The Sleeping Fury* applies here: when you turn and face up to your furies, you find that Eumenides is not a euphemism—that your furies do really wish you well.

47. Dialogue. The enthusiast and the cynic, the Affirmer and the Spirit Who Denies, speak here. The latter is given the last word, and a fair share of the argument; but he is not meant to be the winner.

49. Contra Naturam reflects Everyman's desire to be, just once in a while, the opposite of what he is. The content is deliberately varied between the farce of the Jeremiah and Prufrock stanzas and the more lyrical quality elsewhere.

51. Coat on a Stick. This poem obviously takes off from part of a Yeats stanza in "Sailing to Byzantium." The intention is to begin flippant, colloquial, with a jaunty rhythm; then slow from dactyl to iamb, deepen the tone somewhat, and end with the stark grim finality of the last lines. The end is really stating the urgency of the earlier "clap hands and sing."

53. The Deepening Shades. The same theme, but here treated more lyrically, through metaphor and the symbols of darkness as against music.

54. With Garb of Proof originated in Sir Philip Sidney's sonnet "Come Sleep": ". . . shield me from out the prease/ Of those fierce darts despair at me doth throw."

55. *A Song for Mortimer* is from the scene in King Henry IV, Part I, Act III, scene 1, where the Welsh lady to soothe him sings in her own tongue. This is presumably the English of her Welsh song.

56. "*Mary Morse, Mary Morse*" was first remembered by my brother John and me as a comic bit—from Towanda, Pennsylvania, sixty years ago. Now it seems a good deal deeper, and with some implicit beauty.

58. *To His Mistress, Marvellously Froward* was composed for a *New Statesman* contest (September 17, 1968): problem—to reverse into rebuke the words or theme of a well-known love poem.

59, 61, 62. *Bailiwick, Stwff Ffol*, and *As Compared with the Eskimos* (the latter written after reading Sally Carrighar's *Moonlight at Midday*, whose people are superior to ourselves—they being much nicer, as well as less inept and botchy) all poke some good-natured fun at the Welsh meter *cyhydedd naw ban*.

63. *Camano Island*—a place I had visited, and liked, on Puget Sound, versified from the prose description in Beth Bentley's letter.

65, 68. *Of Redolence* and *Walker at Dusk* are both about Amherst, and both responsive to letters of English Department colleagues, here named.

69. *The Chillblain Indians*. These Chillblain Indians I made up out of whole cloth, or their own red skins. They do not seem a very engaging lot; perhaps the most that can be said is that their Creator must have loved them dearly.

71. *La Cousine*. (After Gérard de Nerval.) A charming little French poem, set for translation in the *New Statesman*'s Week-End Competition #2023. There is enough material in it for at least a half-hour lecture on the problems, immediate and general, with which it confronts the translator—take title, for instance, to begin with.

72. *Arachne, Penelope*. A difficult poem, which began simply with the sight of a red-winged blackbird; then I wanted to counterpoint him with other music makers, neither of whom was quite sure who led, who followed. Hence the weaving girl, Arachne. Then the idea was to set off against them another pair, making music in some different way, with a different kind of assistant. Ah! Penelope, the unweaver;—her

assistant? Nobody. (It is coincidental that Odysseus had told Cyclops his name was Noman.)

74. *Westward Ho!* The title is not without symbolic import. The poem does not scorn some comic stunts, though the general intent is serious: to present the rigors of long adventuring with fury, and to resolve in the only possible way, the comfort of silence.

76. *The Better Theme.* The themes here stated are very simple: that love is better than hate, and music better than jangle. The poem also points out that music does not always come to us as sound; it may present itself as color, motion, act, or even as complete silence.

78. *Said by the Man Who Would Be Well.* This poem starts with simple statement as to time and place, then immediately complicates itself with the entrance of a new figure,—*synergic* being the key word here. It ends, like others, with a good deal of *proest* rhyme.

80. *The Cedar Waxwing.* A beautiful but silly bird killed itself by flying into a western window of our house. My wife found it on the ground, and brought it to me to see and hold for a while before other steps had to be taken.

81. *Finale.* Two things supplied the impulse for this poem: one, a remembered sentence: "The vehicle rolled slowly along the deserted causeway," which needed some explication; and two, the desire to do some further work in one of my favorite Welsh meters, *gwawdodyn hir.*

83. *Transcendence.* An allusion to the song of the morning stars, in an earlier poem, left me feeling the need for fuller treatment of the topic. But in the former instance, *Said by the Man Who Would Be Well,* there was no prospect of continuance or combination. So I had to make up a brand new one.

85. *Five Finger Exercise.* This poem is primarily a five finger stunt, makes a twenty-six-word piece, initial lines in alphabetical order. But I bring in a commentator, attracted by rhyme or image, at more or less appropriate moments.

86. *A Gentle Thing.* This one began as very light verse in praise of two of my medicines, the sound of whose names I liked. But presently, with "ruse" and "rune," which came in because of the long vowel sounds, the poem began to insist on effects of which I had not supposed it capable.

87. *The Screaming Meemies*. There is no excuse in the world for this, written on Twelfth Night, 1969, except for the fatuous delight in one's own idiotic brand of humor.

88. *The Bourgeois*. There was little sense here, to begin with; I was just fooling around, putting rhymes together; they eventually gained some coherence and direction.

89. *To Dread, To Welcome*. This one is simple enough—a presentation of contrast, the dreadful and the pleasant, with some variety in the range.

91. *Adage, Triad*. Each stanza of this poem, in the Welsh *rhupunt* meter, begins with a familiar adage, or corruption thereof; then turns to the Welsh triad; there is no tie-in except in the rhyming of the fourth line with the eighth.

94. *Beowulf Country*. This poem has been expanded from, and detail added to, a much shorter version, by James Murray in his review of my *Lucretius* in the *Long Island Catholic*, 1–16–69.

96. *Identity Crisis* is based on a remark by Thoreau in his Journal to the effect that it was some gain if he got away from the self and could contemplate a more objective thing: in this case a tree.

97. *The Green Land-fall* is a hill slope in Amherst from the foot of the War Memorial to deep left field. No use was made of it except in baseball season. This is one of the loveliest sights I know.

98. *Who Hath Seen?* This poem originated in a letter of Constance Carrier's, in which she wrote of a projected Shactow poem. But another phrase in her letter, the first couplet here, gave me the start of a piece which has turned out rather difficult and complex. Welsh meter, *cywydd devair hirion*.